A souvenir guide

Snowshill Manor and Garden

Gloucestershire

❀ National Trust

The Manor Reborn

Built in the 16th century and extended several times since, Snowshill Manor owes its current form to many people but above all to Charles Paget Wade, who restored it to house his collection, displaying what were to him the essentials of colour, design and craftsmanship.

Nestling at the head of a Cotswold valley, Snowshill Manor has the stature of an idyllic country house. The manor of Snowshill has a long history and was first recorded when the King of Mercia gave it to Winchcombe Abbey in 821 AD. After the dissolution of the monasteries in the 16th century, another monarch, Henry VIII, included it in his dowry to Catherine Parr. After a succession of somewhat less regal owners and tenants, Charles Wade purchased it in 1919. He spent three years restoring it in order that anyone with an interest in design and craftsmanship could marvel at and learn from his collection. The extent of his achievement can be seen today in the huge number of items on show in the twenty rooms of the manor house. By handing the house and the collection to the National Trust in 1951, he ensured that his life's work would continue to be available for others to enjoy.

The Tudor manor

There has been a building on the site since medieval times, possibly since the 9th century. The earliest surviving part of the manor was built around 1550 and comprises the rooms now known as Dragon, Nadir, Ann's, Music and Seraphim. It is likely that this section of the building was once joined to a contemporary building to the south, which was later demolished. In the 1600s, the manor was extended southwards and the attic rooms added. The original entrance was to the west (currently the exit from the house).

'They are rooms to linger in; rooms one must return to; rooms where there is always something to discover; rooms which inspire a thousand fancies.'

Days Far Away. Memories of Charles Paget Wade (1883–1956)

The customised manor

In the early part of the 18th century the house was owned by William Sambach, who added extra rooms on the south-west corner around 1720. He also inserted a new main door in the south front, placing the Sambach arms in the pediment above it – this is now the main entrance to the house. Together with the stone-tiled roof which stretches across the whole of the south front, this development gave the impression of a modest Georgian house. After several further changes of hands, John Small of Clapham took over the property. He was the first of a series of absentee landlords. For the next 150 years, the house was occupied by tenant farmers until Wade bought it in 1919.

Left The various phases of building are apparent on approach to the south front of the manor

Below The interior has not undergone modernisation, its antiquity adding to its atmosphere

Charles Wade – the early years

Born in 1883 in one of the newer London suburbs, Charles Wade was the first child of Paget and Amy Wade, followed soon after by two sisters.

Paget Wade owned sugar estates in the West Indies, which took him away from home for long periods of time. At the age of seven, Charles went to live with his maternal grandmother in Great Yarmouth. Unfortunately, Grannie Spencer was a severe woman who scorned any form of luxury. Charles was largely left to his own devices, finding 'endless things to be discovered'. From a sketch by the young Charles of Grannie's Drawing Room, it would appear she was something of a collector herself.

Education

Charles was a reluctant pupil and found he had no time for schooling. In the book *Days Far Away* he wrote, 'I find I have learnt very little from books … a lot from pictures, but most from objects and craftsmen.'

After leaving school, Charles was articled to an architect in Ipswich, a town that contained 'much of architectural interest', a harbour and also markets and antique shops that fed Charles' burgeoning interest in collecting. Also, despite a clause in his articles prohibiting him from frequenting playhouses and taverns, the Lyceum Theatre became a favourite haunt, where Charles' fondness for the theatrical was indulged.

Towards the end of 1911, his father died. His inheritance included a share in his father's businesses, particularly on the island of St Kitts. This was to provide him with an income and the resources to concentrate on the collection he had been assembling since the age of seven.

Housing the collection

Wade had been looking for a home for his growing collection, which was then housed in his mother's house in Suffolk. During his military service he saw a notice about the sale by auction of Snowshill Manor. Once he was demobilised, he sought out the manor and bought it. It was not in good condition but, as he wrote, 'at least it hadn't been spoilt by modern additions'. With his background and training as an architect, he embarked on a programme of renovation. Stone was extracted from a nearby disused quarry to repair the house; new and renovated panelling was obtained and fitted; much else was restored, all the time 'taking great care to preserve the beautiful old work in the house'. A new garden was designed and constructed where previously there had been a farmyard.

Above A sketch by the young Charles of Grannie's Drawing Room

Left Charles Wade as a young boy

THE SNOWSHILL MANOR ESTATE, SNOWSHILL, near Broadway, Worcs, in eight lots, including a fine OLD COTSWOLD MANOR HOUSE, as illustrated above, and 215 acres, a capital Hill Farm and 246 acres, a Tudor Cottage Residence and five acres, and several old cottages capable of conversion into week-end cottages.— Illustrated particulars from G. H. BAYLEY & SONS, 4, Promenade, Cheltenham.

A house not a home

The restored manor house provided enough space for a lifetime's collection but Wade himself did not live there – instead he refurbished the adjoining cottage as his living quarters. The house also provided a stage for entertaining his friends, especially for dramatic re-enactments of life in the 18th and early 19th centuries. Modern conveniences such as electricity or gas were not wanted. In fact, modernity was strongly discouraged; even lighting and heating were provided by traditional means.

Service in France

In 1917 Charles Wade was serving with the Royal Engineers in France when his artistic temperament nearly got him into trouble. He had transformed the orderly room by adding hessian lining, hanging pictures and making a cupboard for military papers. Pressured by his officer to make the room look more functional, he added some maps but in neat frames and with a little colouring so they did not detract from 'the cosiness of the room'. The effect was apparently successful: a visiting general congratulated Wade on achieving so much with so little. Also during his service in France, another event occurred that would determine the course of his life. One day he read about the sale of Snowshill Manor in *Country Life*. As soon as he was discharged, he went to view the property and bought it.

Architect and artist

Below Ink plan and three elevations of 'Design for one floor cottage' by Wade

Right Watercolour drawing by Wade marked 'illustration for child's book, C Wade, June 1904'

Opposite A watercolour by Wade, marked 'The Dovecot'

Charles Wade made architecture his profession, a calling which made good use of his skills in draughtsmanship as well as his imagination and interest in design.

After qualifying as an architect, Wade went to work for the partnership of Parker & Unwin on designs for Hampstead Garden Suburb. His influence on the Hampstead cottages was 'so profound that he deserves special mention', according to one colleague.

Drawing on detail

But his interests were broader than just the design of buildings. He spent much of his spare time drawing and painting. His first published drawings were illustrations for Raymond Unwin's *Town Planning in Practice* in 1909. After he left Parker & Unwin in 1911, he exhibited at the Whitechapel Art Gallery and went on to provide many finely detailed illustrations for *Bruges: A Record and an Impression* (a book by Mary Stratton) and also for *The Spirit of the House,* a book written by his friend Kate Murray.

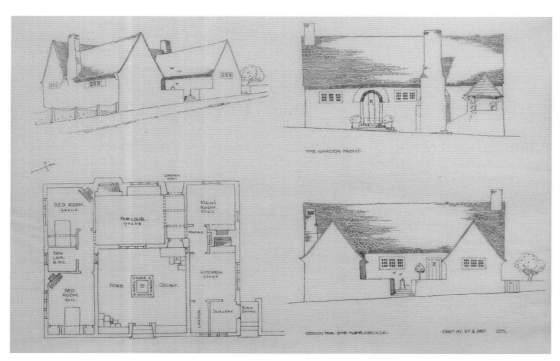

The Arts and Crafts Movement

Responding to the rapid growth of industrialisation in the second half of the 19th century, John Ruskin, William Morris and others put forward ideas about design and craftsmanship. This grew into the Arts and Crafts Movement. Their principles – expressed as a unity of design, joy in labour, individualism and regionalism – can be recognised in Charles Wade's own thinking about the 'essentials of design, colour and craftsmanship'. This is not surprising as Wade associated with several of the leading lights of the Arts and Crafts Movement.

Barry Parker and his brother-in-law Raymond Unwin put emphasis on the functionalism of design. They attracted several important commissions, including one from Joseph Rowntree, another for the garden city at Letchworth and also the master plan for Hampstead Garden Suburb. Unwin led the Hampstead project from 1907 to 1915 with Edwin Lutyens as consultant and involving a number of other distinguished architects, including M. H. Baillie Scott.

Not only did Wade share many ideals with the Arts and Crafts architects and designers, his arrival in Gloucestershire followed the path that several in the movement had trodden to the Cotswolds, especially to Chipping Campden. Later, Gordon Russell established a business manufacturing his own designs of furniture in Broadway. His use of machines for small-scale production, whilst making good design available to a wider audience, tended to undercut the work of craftsmen, an inherent conflict that had concerned Morris many years previously.

A life-long passion

Charles Wade's interest in beautifully designed and skilfully made objects began at an early age. This fascination inspired a collection that would become his life's work.

The seven-year-old Charles' introduction to the pleasures of beautiful objects came from his grandmother, who owned a Chinese cabinet filled with all manner of wondrous things. This was only opened on Sundays when the young Wade was allowed to peek in.

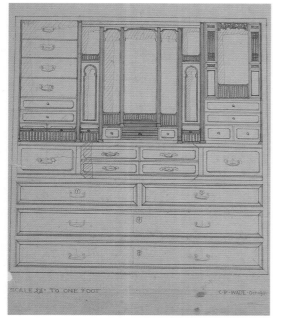

Stimulated by the sight of these treasures he decided he would make his own collection, his first 'find' being a small shrine of St Michael made of bone which cost him 18 weeks' pocket money. Despite being told he was 'wasting his money on rubbish', he carried on collecting, maintaining the enthusiasm he had for his collection as a boy right the way through his adult life.

Finds from afar

His expeditions to hunt out new finds led him to country towns and large cities, and occasionally abroad, in the company of one of his friends, especially Commander Fred Hart or Professor Sir Albert Richardson. At first he collected simple items, mainly by English makers but, over time, his interests broadened to include European furniture and exotic items from the East.

Noted visitors

Word of his collection spread amongst literary and artistic circles, many of whom were prepared to make the journey into the wilds of Gloucestershire to experience it and its unusual guardian. Some recorded their excitement: J. B. Priestley wrote, 'The owner, in the most charming fashion, conducted us over his house.... I have never seen such a collection outside a public museum.' John Buchan wrote, 'The house inside was truly amazing, for Mr Wade was a collector in the widest sense of the word.' Other visitors who committed their impressions to paper included John Betjeman, Virginia Woolf and Graham Greene. Wade even received royalty, with Queen Mary visiting on two occasions.

Left A drawing by Charles Wade of his grandmother's cabinet

Opposite Among the many items on show, the visitor will see items from the distant past and some from distant lands

The joys of collecting

Travelling to many parts of the country in search of his 'finds', Charles Wade bought from street markets and from dealers' shops and many other, less obvious places. Some of the people he encountered knew the value of what they were selling, but others wanted far more than Wade was prepared to pay.

Wade claimed that the activity of collecting gave him 'such a wonderful opportunity for a wider view of humanity', especially when this brought him into contact with the craftsmen themselves, such as one old weaver who had made Edward VII's coronation robes – his skills were of the highest order but 'not appreciated by his wife'.

Originally Wade's intention had been to collect English-made objects, but he found only a limited number made use of colour, so he turned his attention to items from Spain and Italy, Persia and the Far East. Transporting his finds back to Snowshill presented a much greater challenge than it would today. One story told is of Wade being arrested in London's Oxford Street for wearing a suit of armour he had just bought, because that was the only way he could carry it home.

No matter how enjoyable the hunt for a new piece, the task of restoring it in his workshop provided even greater pleasure. Removing layers of dirt and making careful repairs, Wade made yet more discoveries about the items he brought to Snowshill. Using a range of materials and techniques, he became a skilled craftsman, though he professed only to being a 'Jack of Many Trades' and 'Master of Some'.

Collecting companions

Two of Charles Wade's friends stand out as sharing his passion for collecting, taking part in many joint expeditions with him – Lieutenant Commander Fred Hart and Professor Sir Albert Richardson.

Albert Richardson was a contemporary of Wade's, an eminent architect whose commercial practice produced many notable buildings. Richardson also held the Chair of Architecture at the Bartlett School, London, where his lectures were renowned for their impromptu graphic demonstrations, a skill which he also used to entertain parties at Snowshill Manor. He had a long association with the Royal Academy, which culminated in him becoming President in 1954. He was knighted in 1956.

Shared interests

Such a glittering career may seem a long way removed from the somewhat eccentric world of Wade, but they shared a particular interest in English domestic architecture from the 17th to the 19th century. Richardson also liked to dress in 18th-century costume when at home. He lived in an 18th-century house at Ampthill in Bedfordshire, where he kept a large collection of furniture and art, and where he refused to have electricity installed (until his wife persuaded him otherwise). Richardson's grandson recorded how 'Snowshill had a strange effect on my grandfather…. His vivacity and outrageousness seemed to quadruple the moment the car nosed its way into Wade's courtyard.'

Friend and curator

Fred Hart was on leave from the Navy when he first met Wade, soon after the latter moved to Snowshill, and their common interests developed into a strong friendship. After retiring from the Navy in 1924, Hart bought a house in Chipping Campden and together he and Wade began visiting shops and attending sales, first local ones and then further afield, their various finds crammed into Hart's car. On some occasions, Hart would walk the seven miles from Chipping Campden to Snowshill bringing with him some of his home-made wine, spend the afternoon and evening there and then walk home again. In 1930, they toured a number of European countries by car, adding to their collections. After the National Trust took over Snowshill Manor, Hart was asked to become honorary curator in the interregnum before the permanent curator took up his post.

Left Professor Sir Albert Richardson (1880–1964), by Lewis Morley, 1961

Far left Charles Wade posing in Cromwellian costume. For all his apparent eccentricity he found friends with similar passions

Charles Wade – the later years

An unconventional character

Charles Wade's customary attire was long coat, knee breeches, stockings and silver-buckled shoes with a loose shirt. He rarely varied his wardrobe, no matter what the season or occasion. Wade was always clean shaven with long hair parted in the middle, curled about his ears. One contemporary remembered him as 'unconventional, even in Hampstead which in those days … attracted many unconventional characters'.

After he reached his fiftieth year, Charles Wade seems to have become more concerned about the future of his collection. He approached the National Trust which, in 1938, agreed in principle to accept it as a gift. Encouraged by the security that this provided, Wade stepped up his efforts, more than doubling the size of the collection.

In 1946, to the surprise of most of his acquaintances, Wade married Mary Graham, when she was 44 and he was 63. Mary McEwen Gore Graham was born in 1902 in Worcester, the daughter of a vicar. During World War II she worked as an inspector of utility furniture at Gordon Russell's factory in Broadway and had sought Wade out during one of the occasions when his garden was open to the public.

After they married, they lived in the cottage at Snowshill for five years before moving to St Kitts in 1951. In 1956, during a holiday in England, Wade was taken ill and died at Evesham. Mary survived him by many years, retiring to Broadway where she lived to the ripe old age of 96. Charles and Mary are buried together with his sisters in the churchyard at Snowshill.

Above Mary Wade

Right Charles Paget Wade, c.1940

Opposite An ivory nymph suspended in one of the niche cupboards in the Entrance Hall

A valuable collection

Professor Sir Albert Richardson, Charles' close friend and President of the Royal Academy, encapsulated the value of Wade's achievement: 'It is not a junk shop, it is a serious collection which will be of utmost use to students in the future.'

'Let Nothing Perish'

There is much to see on a tour around Snowshill Manor, from the various phases of building visible on the outside to the vast and varied array of objects assembled inside. In this guidebook you'll find just some of Snowshill's highlights, but you may find you need to come back again and again to see it all.

The south front is approached by way of the small lodges, formerly used as stables, and through two forecourts, separated by a fine pair of gate piers of *c.1720*. These piers represent the original road boundary of the property.

From here the front has a handsome and, at first glance, a regular appearance. But on closer inspection, variations become apparent – the windows on the right have mullions and transoms, whilst those on the left are sash windows. These styles reflect the different ages of construction: the part on the right is the earlier (*c.1600*) building; that on the left is the later extension (1720). Over the door are the arms of William Sambach, who was responsible for the form of the south front today.

Nothing wasted

The first hint of Charles Wade is seen even before entering the house: the post-box to the left of the door carries his coat of arms together with his motto *NEQUID PEREAT*, which means 'Let nothing perish'. This phrase not only reflects the purpose of the collection but also the way in which Wade went about his work, whether restoring a broken object or using scraps of paper for drawing, including both sides of each sheet. This is a marked contrast with modern attitudes, where consumer goods may be recycled but rarely repaired, and basic materials are used once and thrown away.

Wade's humour

Once inside the front door, other versions of the coats of arms can be seen. All of these were painted by Wade, who developed his own coat of arms as an ironic expression of his genealogy. His friend, Mrs Alison Coates, recorded that 'their placing, with the others in the house, was a typical "leg-pull", of which he was very fond'.

Opposite **The south front of the house in summer**

Above **One of Charles Wade's versions of his coat of arms**

Turquoise Room

Ground Floor

The wooden panelling and cornices in this room are original, dating from the 1720 extension. This room was coloured to reflect those used in the garden furniture, for which Charles Wade created his own colour – Wade blue. It is worth taking time to acclimatise to the low levels of lighting in order to take in the enormous range and variety of Wade's collection.

Below The Turquoise Room with original softwood panelling, repainted by Charles Wade

Right The Dog of Fo statue in the fireplace

In the 1940s, many beautiful items made in Japan and China were available relatively cheaply on the English market. Much of the contents of the Turquoise Room were purchased by Wade at that time. His favourite object in the whole house was the Japanese figure in the cabinet in the left-hand corner, the Maker of Masks (the masks concerned being for use in a form of Japanese theatre called *No*). This wonderful figure, carved from solid wood, is so lifelike that the veins are clearly visible on the arms and legs and the muscles stand out in full detail; it is so precisely made that it features real human hair. This is one of a set of figures made by the Japanese carver Hananuma in the 19th century; another from the same set, the Peddler of Baskets, is next to the door.

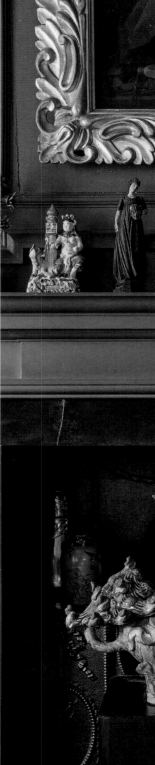

Furniture

On the left-hand wall, the magnificent cabinet is in a Venetian style that was popular in the 16th century, although this one is thought to date from about 1850. Wade's friend, Professor Sir Albert Richardson, found this in a shop in Taunton. The front is tortoiseshell, inlayed with brass and semi-precious stones. In and around the cabinet are various Chinese and Japanese objects, most of which were also purchased in Britain.

To the right of the entrance is a Cantonese black lacquer cabinet with gold decoration based on the design of a Buddhist shrine which holds a variety of Chinese artefacts, including an opium press of ivory inlaid with birds and flowers in mother-of-pearl, obtained in Cheltenham.

Models

H.M.S. *Romulus* is the largest of the model ships in the house; in fact it was too large to be carried upstairs to its intended home in the attic. This late 18th-century model displays *Romulus* in great detail, reflecting the high level of skill that went into making it. It was one of two models Wade purchased in Towcester in 1948 for £110.

From the Orient

Snarling at you from the hearth is a Dog of Fo, the guardian of Buddhist temples in China. On the wall to the left of it hangs a Japanese clock which was given to Wade by a furniture remover who had been told by a client 'not to bother with that junk in the attic'. Wade used to keep the Japanese wind god, now hanging on the right-hand wall, over the forge in his workshop in order to 'provide a draught'.

Right Detail of the Italian cabinet

H.M.S. *Romulus*

The full-size version was launched in 1777 at Bucklers Hard, carrying 44 guns. In 1779 she was part of a squadron under Admiral Arbuthnot that attacked and captured Charleston, South Carolina. In 1781, whilst in passage to Chesapeake Bay, she encountered and was captured by the French.

They renamed her *La Résolution* and continued to use her for several years until she was paid off in 1789 at Mauritius, ending her days as a hulk.

Meridian
Admiral

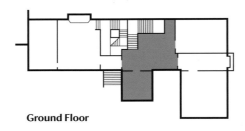

Ground Floor

Meridian

Charles Wade gave names to each of the rooms in the manor, to denote their position, decoration or contents. He painted their names on the lintels over the doorways. Thus Meridian is the room in the centre of the house. The walls are lined in oak panelling, some of which dates from the Tudor period.

The subdued lighting in Meridian is just what Wade wanted to make the 'golds and glints of polished metal' stand out. The atmosphere of an 'ancient continental church' with a golden shrine lit by tapers would display to best effect the 16th-century reliquary bust of St Ignatius of Loyola, the founder of the Jesuit movement, which is opposite the entrance.

Furniture

Wade did not want furniture to stand out in a room, preferring 'furnishings that would make an attractive series of rooms pictorially'. The red cabinet is decorated in tortoiseshell with ebony mouldings, and houses a gilt figure in the central recess of the door. This early 18th-century Italian cabinet was purchased from a bric-a-brac stall in Worcester, where Wade saw it on the pavement.

In contrast to the religious objects, the red leather hall-porter's chair is much more utilitarian. The sedan chair opposite was used at the royal Château of Marly, near Versailles. It is decorated with the Royal Emblems of France and has the number seventeen painted on the back, reflecting its role in transporting visitors to the château.

Left A chased gilt figure in the door of the Italian red tortoiseshell cabinet

Niche crafts

Two cupboards, on either side of the passage way into Meridian, contain a collection of carvings made from animal bones by French prisoners during the Napoleonic Wars. The prisoners would form groups to make the models, each man specialising in a particular component. Ship models (such as can be seen in Admiral) are very fine examples of this craft, impressively accurate given the circumstances.

Admiral

This small room houses many nautical and scientific objects. It was part of the 1720 extension to the house and is essentially unaltered, except for the bow-fronted cupboard which Charles Wade introduced to balance the diagonal fireplace on the left.

Many practical devices have their own particular beauty, something that Wade appreciated, recognising the craftsmanship that went into making them. Here there are many instruments for making precise measurements, such as the position and direction of ships, atmospheric pressure, the time of day, the height of buildings or the distance of a target.

Astronomical aids

Celestial relationships could be explored using an armillary sphere: an early 19th-century example is on the floor. This one has several rings displaying the signs of the zodiac and the positions of the planets. A later development, the orrery, incorporates a clockwork-drive: several examples of this are also on the floor.

Above Detail of an armillary heliocentric sphere, French, 1810–20

Right Admiral contains a large collection of nautical items including globes, model ships and 18th- and 19th-century naval swords

Zenith

Ground Floor

As a small boy, Charles Wade lived with his grandmother. In her drawing room was an old Chinese cabinet of black and gold lacquer. He recalled, 'this was my greatest joy and its fascination never failed'. So this cabinet has pride of place in Zenith – metaphorically the high point of the house.

The treasures housed in Grannie's cabinet were locked away all week, the doors only being opened on Sundays: 'As they opened, out came the fragrance of camphor, then the interior of this Enchanted Golden Palace was revealed, a Palace fit for the greatest Mandarin'. The young Charles longed to be allowed to stand on a chair 'so as to be able to see into all its innermost recesses, the whole reflected many times in the mirrors set each side in the forecourts'.

Furniture

The shape of Grannie's cabinet is intended to represent a Buddhist shrine, with many drawers and pavilions inside, concealed by sliding screens and internal partitions. Such cabinets were imported from China by the East India Company, often filled with tea. This one was purchased in Norwich by Wade's great-grandfather, Augustine Bulwer.

The cabinet was filled with old family treasures, including a wax angel with golden wings for a Christmas tree, his great-grandfather's pocket compass in a red leather case, a pair of silver spectacles in a shagreen (dyed shark or ray skin) case and much more besides. Most of these treasures are still in the cabinet, plus others that Wade added, including several finely made Chinese and Japanese artefacts.

Below The elaborate locking mechanism of an armada chest

Furnishings

To the right of the window is an eight-day English tavern clock. This dates from about 1785 when such clocks were used in coaching inns, market halls and other places as public timepieces.

Under the clock is a 17th-century iron strong box (there is another between the windows). These boxes were made in Germany and served as safes, often containing elaborate locking mechanisms. They are referred to as 'armada chests', although there is some doubt as to whether the Spanish Armada would have been able to use anything so heavy. Nevertheless, Wade made a joke out of the name by putting some bowls in this one, an allusion to the famous story of the game of bowls that Sir Francis Drake finished before tackling the approaching Armada.

Below Grannie's cabinet takes pride of place in Zenith

Front Stairs and Corridor
Green Room

Front Stairs and Corridor

These stairs provided access to the new rooms added in 1720. At the top of the stairs is a Latin inscription: 'For me today – for him tomorrow – after that, who knows?' Charles Wade felt that the corridor was a 'gaunt and lofty alley', so he improved it by fitting a curved ceiling.

At the head of the stairs is a portrait of Wade, age 68, painted by his friend Mrs K. Browning, the wife of the vicar of St Kitts. Wade commissioned this to encourage her efforts as an artist. Several other items here hark back to Wade's ancestors, but one of the more intriguing pieces is the side of a coach decorated with the arms of the Countess Cowper, a close friend of Victorian Prime Minister Lord Palmerston. It contains an oil portrait of a man whose identity is not known.

Pictures

Further down the corridor, the pictures in oval frames are watercolours of Frances and Edward Bulwer, two of the children of Wade's great-great-great-grandfather. The small barrel organ at the end of the corridor once belonged to Wade's great-great-grandmother, Bridget Lloyd.

Right Detail of a Chinese screen in the Green Room

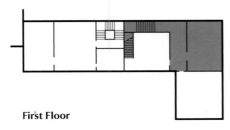

First Floor

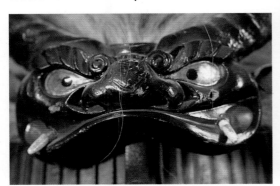

Green Room

Here Charles Wade created the most atmospheric room in the manor. He allowed creeper to cover the windows, creating a gloomy setting in which a group of Japanese Samurai could be glimpsed approaching. Today, the curtains are kept closed so that the darkness conveys a similarly threatening scene.

The discovery of some of these suits of Samurai armour was extraordinary, even for Wade: 'One day wanting a washer for a tap, I called at a tiny shop in Cheltenham; it was so small, a sink and six taps filled its window. Standing there, by the counter, was a set of Samurai armour! The owner said "I have some more in the yard" and out there he pulled off a tarpaulin and produced six complete suits that he had had for 26 years.' Not surprisingly, the shopkeeper's wife would not let him keep them in the house.

Wade already had one suit of Samurai armour which was kept in a chest because he could not find a satisfactory place for it in the manor. Then, in a cellar off the Charing Cross Road in London, he found many more pieces from which he reconstructed four more suits. In total, he brought together 28 suits of armour but only eleven are currently on display.

Setting the stage
Eventually, he decided to make an oriental room at the manor. Using many other Japanese and Chinese items, Wade aimed to achieve an impression of the Far East in a bygone age. The saddles, stirrups and *hibachi* (a traditional heating device) on the floor might have been used by the Samurai. The large Buddhist shrine against the left wall dates from the 18th century. The masks on the wall opposite were made for the *No* theatre.

Below right **Fearsome-looking armour of a Samurai warrior**

Below left **Close view of a Samurai helmet**

Costume Room

First Floor

This room had a westerly aspect, but the three windows on that side had been blocked up before Charles Wade's arrival. He chose not to re-open them, preferring the light from the south-facing windows. Here Wade kept his costume collection, some of which is periodically on display, along with items that provide some insight into the man himself.

At the age of fourteen, Charles Wade started his collection of costumes with two Georgian suits, which he purchased in Norwich Market. The colour and craftsmanship of English costumes in the 18th century were clearly to his taste but the collection is not limited to English garments, including as it does items from the Balkans, Italy and the Far East. Nor was it a static collection – Wade was fond of dressing up in old costumes, and he and his friends would often do this for their dramatic performances.

In all Wade brought together 2,250 pieces of 18th- and 19th-century apparel, including men's and women's fashions, court costume, gowns, crinolines, dresses and suits, hats and bonnets, shoes, bags and other accessories, mostly from the period before the sewing machine allowed industrial methods of production.

J. B. Priestley was impressed with the scale of the collection which 'could have dressed whole opera companies'.

Wade wanted the costumes to be kept at Snowshill but, because of the sheer volume of space required to display them properly, most of the costume collection has been moved to Berrington Hall near Leominster. Some of it is on open display there; costume enthusiasts can make an appointment to see other items of the collection at Berrington Hall.

Cloisters
Wade had planned to build a cloister building for his costume collection in a garden area to the north of the manor. Wade's sketches for the cloisters survive in the manor archives but they were sadly never built, possibly due to lack of funds or the outbreak of World War II.

Below Charles Wade's architectural drawing of the Cloisters

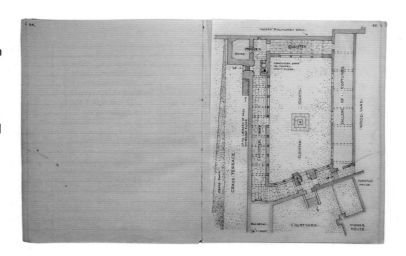

Models

On top of the cabinets are some of the buildings from an outdoor model village that Wade built in Hampstead between 1907 and 1914. This was later developed into the village of Wolf's Cove which was set up in the garden at Snowshill. The Bassett-Lowke clockwork train that ran through the village can be seen underneath the cabinets.

Charlie told us, with a wicked twinkle in his eye, that once Queen Mary ... said she would like to visit Snowshill. He sent a frantic telegram to his mother to come and help him. He also got some pretty young girls ... to dress up in some of his beautiful antique costumes. These girls formed a tableaux in the room where he had his antique garments, and after Queen Mary entered the room they curtseyed in unison and Charlie says the Queen was quite startled – she thought they were waxworks – she also asked Charlie for one of his antique teapots ... I wonder where that teapot is now.'

Above **Charles Wade and friends in costume**

Letter from Doreen May, 24 October 1985

Grey Room

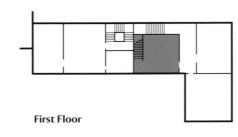

First Floor

During the initial restoration of the manor, this room was painted grey but the sight from the window of the dovecote in the garden was a reminder of the white dove on the Noah's Ark toy (upstairs in Seventh Heaven), which suggested another name for this room – Noah's Dove.

Charles Wade never lived in the manor but sometimes visitors would stay in this room. The canopied bed is Flemish and dates from about 1700.

Furniture
To the right of the bed, the Chinese cabinet displays a shrine-like interior and many drawers, decorated with landscape scenes. As with the other cabinets in the house, Wade kept a variety of beautiful items in it, as well as some oddities. There are lacquer boxes, bowls and jars, jade and silver, and Japanese and Chinese ivory, much of it displaying fine and intricate carving. Wade would open the cabinets, then select certain items which he would ceremonially hand to his guests so that they could experience not just the sight but also the feel of the objects.

Other items
On the window sill is a replica 19th-century pill-making machine, representing important developments of the day, enabling precise measurement and accurate cutting and shaping of the pills. Beside it are some of the last objects purchased by Wade: the carvings from a Sicilian *carretto*, a highly decorated horse-drawn cart, were only delivered after his death.

Left Grey Room

Right Close view of a 17th-century crewel-work bed-hanging

Mermaid

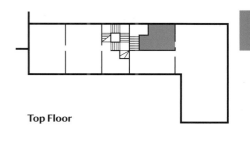

Top Floor

The exhibits in this room reflect some of the formative stages in Wade's life, including his upbringing in Great Yarmouth. The bench at the top of the stairs may be used by visitors, although you may not be so pleased to know its original purpose was for butchering pigs.

One of Wade's great friends, Kate Murray, was an author. He used his artistic skills to illustrate one of her books and also made various amusements for her daughter, Elizabeth, such as the smaller of the two doll's houses here. Elizabeth's photograph is fixed on the wall above.

The front of the larger doll's house has been removed to show the inside. There is a variety of rooms, including a grocer's shop in the lower right-hand room. This shop was the basis for one of the favourite games that the young Charles played with his sisters. He imagined the shop was kept by one Robert Taylor, who provided a variety of goods to the doll's houses belonging to his sisters.

Right Large doll's house complete with grocer's shop and proprietor, Robert Taylor

A Hundred Wheels

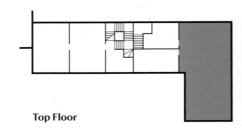

Top Floor

The growing need for personal transport in the 19th century stimulated a great deal of innovation on the part of craftsmen. Charles Wade sought out their products, especially bicycles and prams, as examples of developments from the days before mass production.

Hanging from the rafters are three Penny Farthing bicycles – the name refers to the hugely different sizes of the wheels, reflecting the sizes of two coins, the penny and the farthing. The large front wheel would have made mounting and dismounting quite a challenge, yet Wade is known to have ridden these bicycles around the courtyard. The largest one also demonstrates a neat solution to the problem of cycling by night – an oil lamp is suspended inside the front wheel. Underneath these are twelve two-wheeled 'boneshakers' (bicycles that were propelled by pedals on the front wheels) as well as a restored example of an earlier type, the 'hobby horse', that was propelled by the rider using his feet on the ground.

The three- and four-wheeled velocipedes against the far wall form a unique collection. The three-wheeled example, the 'Experiment' built in 1840, was the first that could free-wheel. After searching for several years, Wade also found a four-wheeled model, known as the 'postman's carriage', in a shop in Framlingham.

The shop's owner was away sick, so Wade was able to persuade his son to sell it, against his better judgement: 'I shall catch it from Dad'. Whether he did is not recorded. Right up in the apex of the roof is a very unusual example of a child's quadricycle.

Many of the craftsmen who made boneshakers also made baby-carriages, and at the far end of the room is a rare collection of seven, very early perambulators. A shopkeeper in Wymondham Market had written to Wade about a three-wheeled version that he had found but, by the time Wade was able to visit the shop, the letter and the pram had both been forgotten. Fortunately, Wade was allowed to search the sheds behind the shop until 'the very pram rolled out between us'.

Toys

Five children's toy carts alongside are worth close inspection for their fine detailing, having been modelled on horse-drawn carriages, right down to the necessary springs. There is also much fine detail on the 23 model farm wagons on the shelf – demonstrating the subtle differences between the wagons of the different counties that were still in use in the late 1930s. Their maker, H. R. Waiting, had been commissioned by Wade, but unfortunately died before completing the county set. Wade painted the finished wagons himself.

Right **A Hundred Wheels**

YARMOUTH BLOATERS and KIPPERS

Seventh Heaven

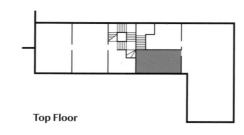

Top Floor

Charles Wade thought of Seventh Heaven as a state 'only to be attained in childhood, before schools and schoolmasters have been able to destroy the greatest of all treasures, imagination'. One of his favourite parts of the collection was the toys and nursery furniture, which represent 'a Kingdom beyond the ken of grown-ups'.

Before the days of television, optical toys, such as those on the shelf to the left of the window, could be used to present novel sights, such as views of scenes by night and day, or a kaleidoscope of colours. On the lower shelf more traditional toys include a toy trumpet and a jumping jack.

Finding ways of minding baby seems to have been a stimulus for invention for many years; several different solutions to the problem can be seen here. One such is a wooden frame on legs with a sliding restraint to hold the child in place. The type with a pole was introduced in the 16th century whilst the one on castors was a 17th-century development and bears a strong resemblance to some in use today.

In the early days of the railways, there was a wider choice of seating. The wooden train on the floor faithfully conveys these differences, with the first-class accommodation having curtains and a luggage rack on the roof, second class also having a roof but open windows, whilst third-class passengers had to ride in open wagons.

Beside the train, the furniture van drawn by a pair of horses was one of Wade's own toys; this was used with Robert Taylor's shop now in Mermaid.

On the far shelf is a 19th-century wooden ark, made in the Black Forest, from which Noah's dove can be seen flying. To the right is a doll's house that had once belonged to Wade's mother: 'How inviting it looked, the front so trim, so prim.'

'These toys grew up with us … lived with us so long it was impossible to think of parting with them. They seemed as solid and everlasting as Queen Victoria.'

Days Far Away. Memories of Charles Paget Wade (1883–1956)

Childhood memories

Charles Wade retained strong memories of his childhood. The three great events in the calendar, as far as he was concerned, were the annual visit to the travelling circus, November the fifth and, greatest of all, Christmas. Not only did Christmas mean presents and decorations, but also involved the pantomime, sometimes at school but, on one memorable occasion, at Drury Lane in London, where Wade was introduced to a whole new world of theatre. After you have descended from Seventh Heaven and returned to the ground floor, you will see how this theatricality developed in Wade's later life, most notably in the performances staged in the dramatically named Salamander and Dragon.

Above A baby walker or 'minder'

Far left Noah's Ark with model animals made in the mid-19th century in the Black Forest

Left The front façade of the doll's house that once belonged to Charles Wade's mother

Top Royal
Top Gallant

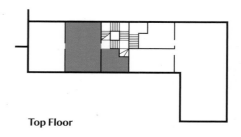

Top Floor

Top Royal

The position of this room at the top of the house is reflected in its name, a reference to the upper part of the main mast of a sailing ship. The theme of this room, and its neighbours, is country crafts, activities that were fast disappearing at the time that Charles Wade was building his collection. Here is a snapshot of history staged as a cobbler's shop.

The cobbler of Yoxford, Sam Thurlow, served his customers from this workbench. Here he produced new shoes and repaired old ones using the lasts (or patterns) modelled on their feet. As each last carried the customer's name and was adapted over time to accommodate the corns and bunions of their feet, 'around the walls of the shop was recorded some intimate village history'. Some finished shoes are on the floor.

Other long-gone country occupations are represented by the clamps, which were used to hold gloves whilst stitching, and various items of lace-making equipment, including bobbins and bobbin-winders, lace pillows and an embroidery frame on the bench.

Country crafts
The Wade family moved to the village of Yoxford, close to the Suffolk coast, in 1896. The contrast with the London suburbs delighted the young Charles, especially the 'unchanged countryside' and the range of characters to be seen in the village – servants from the large houses, local fishermen, as well as various craftsmen, including the carpenter and cobbler. The village shop stocked a fascinating variety of supplies, not only groceries but also draperies and hardware. The parish fire engine was kept in its own little house opposite the pub – when needed it would be pulled by two horses but any pumping of water would have to be done by hand (two examples of such fire engines can be seen in the Sancta Maria Byre in the garden).

Right Cobbler's bench and full set of tools used by Sam Thurlow of Yoxford

Top Gallant

The names of this room and the next one are also from the upper masts of a sailing ship and the theme of country crafts continues – here, spinning and weaving.

Small-scale cloth-making industries had largely disappeared by the 1920s so, when Charles Wade found a silk mill and loom, he was keen to acquire them. The silk warping mill on the right-hand side belonged to Miss Pleasance Webb of Sudbury in Suffolk. Miss Webb used it, together with the driving machine close by, to produce silk for her companion, Miss Alice Howsden, whose loom is next door in Mizzen.

The spinning wheels take many different forms depending on the type of fibre to be spun: some have single wheels, others double wheels; some are arranged vertically, others horizontally. Beside them are bobbin frames, wool-winders and machines for measuring the amount of yarn produced. Other villagers would also need to measure their goods, such as the baker who would use one of the steelyards to weigh out his bread; farmers would use beam-scales such as those on the window sill and over the door into Mizzen.

A turret clock by W. Jones of Abingdon, 1803, hangs by the door. This type of clock, often used in churches, has no hands but strikes the hours. Wade painted a scale on the wall to show the time by a pointer on the descending weight. The riddles about time are from the writings of English poet and novelist Nicholas Breton (1545–1626).

Right A horizontal spinning wheel from Holland and vertical wheel from the North West of England

Mizzen

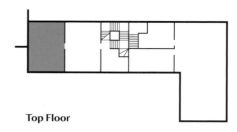

Top Floor

This room continues the display of spinning and weaving machines plus some long-vanished domestic appliances.

The hand loom in the centre of the room is the one that Miss Alice Howden used for weaving fine silks in Sudbury in partnership with Pleasance Webb: some examples of the woven fabrics that were produced can be seen in a frame attached to the roof beam. Here are several more spinning wheels including a great wheel, the earliest sort of spinning wheel thought to have been developed from an Indian type. By the far wall is an unusual musical notation board, designed specifically to enable

a blind composer to record his work.

The box mangle on the right was used to press freshly washed linen. By placing rocks in the box on the top and moving this back and forth over the linen, large items could be dried and pressed very efficiently. But it needed two people to operate, so was only used in very large households – this one was obtained from a house in Chipping Campden where it was still in use when Wade found it. Beside it is a photograph of Dottie Hands, Wade's housekeeper. Mrs Hands was devoted to Wade, even to the point of keeping a watchful eye on the gate and telling any uninvited strangers that 'it's private, every bit of it'.

Bottom A selection of shuttles

Below Dottie Hands operating the box mangle

Old Stairs

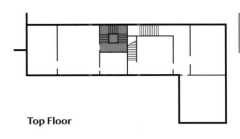
This staircase was built when the house was extended in the 1600s.

Suspended above the stairs is a wooden windlass which was at one time used in the malt house at the Snowshill Arms. Leather fire buckets line the wall, the ones with crests coming from the estate of Lord Henniker.

Clocks

The clock on the left of the door from Top Gallant was made in about 1740 with the unusual feature of a wooden movement and, necessarily, rather coarse teeth. Its dial, also made of wood, is divided just into quarter-hours to suit the single hand.

The large tavern clock on the wall may have come from a servant's hall in a great house as it has a crest painted on the door; it has an eight-day movement. Curiously, the Roman numerals at the nine-o'clock position have been painted the wrong way round.

Continuing the horological theme, on the window sill is some clock-making equipment – a gear cutter and two clock-maker's lathes.

A matter of time

The writer H. J. Massingham described how 'the transformation of the house into something rich and strange was accentuated by the multitude of old clocks … all ticking at once … all pointing to different times, so that the stairways echoed with tickings loud and soft, bass and treble, clear and muffled, fast and slow'. Charles Wade deliberately set the clocks to chime at different times, providing a form of background music for the house. Distracted by this profusion of clocks, Virginia Woolf, visiting Snowshill with John Buchan in 1935, rather crossly recorded that Wade 'pretended to have no watch and so I lost my train'.

Above right **Leather fire buckets**

Ann's Room

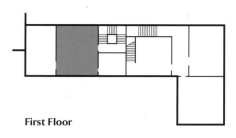

First Floor

In this room, Ann Parsons secretly married Anthony Palmer on St Valentine's eve, 1604. In recognition, Charles Wade marked the date above the door and painted the motto *amor et tussis non celantur*, which means 'Love and a cough are not concealed'.

One of the Snowshill ghosts supposedly walks in here from the Music Room next door. On occasions Wade's friends would stay the night in Ann's Room in the hope of seeing this apparition. One brave girl who did this (it has to be said in the company of her mother) did not see the ghost but later recalled that 'a few notes of music appeared to emanate from the Music Room of their own volition'.

Below Ann's Room

Furniture

The magnificent canopied four-poster bed is almost as old as the tale of Ann's marriage (it was made about 1630). Features which reflect its age include the five holes in the side rails to hold candles during the vigil before a burial and the rope base under the mattress which would have been tightened before use, hence the expression 'sleep tight'. The English oak coffer at the foot of the bed has been draped in a rug typical of the Feraghan area of Persia (modern Iran). On the rug is a box housing a delicate example of quill work which was probably made by nuns in Provence; the central panel shows the Virgin and Child.

Books

As the manor did not have electricity in Wade's time, lighting would have been provided by candles or even rush-lights, some holders for which can be seen in the hearth. Whether these would have provided enough light to read by is questionable, but some of the few books in the manor are here – these being 17th- and 18th-century religious and legal texts.

Fireside furniture

Without central heating, in fact without very much heating at all, the wing backs on the rocking chairs would have provided useful protection against draughts. The hearth contains a collection of cooking implements, including several iron stands for toasting bread, a tripod for supporting pots and a skillet with a long handle, but it is unlikely these were used here.

From this room, one doorway leads to the Music Room, the other to Seraphim.

The elopement of Ann and Anthony

Ann Parsons was a young orphan and heiress, who had an affair with a 20-year-old servant, Anthony Palmer, even though she had been contracted to marry someone else. On St Valentine's eve 1604, the young couple ran away together, coming to Snowshill Manor which was then owned by a relative of Ann's. Here they were married by a local vicar at around midnight, afterwards travelling on to Chipping Campden. The elopement was discovered and Ann was retrieved by her guardian but Palmer did not give up and took her away again. In due course, Palmer and his accomplices were charged with abducting Ann and with contriving an unlawful marriage. The case was tried by the secretive Star Chamber but its decision is not recorded.

The final twist to this story was that Charles Wade sent a sample of timber from a beam in Ann's Room to a medium in Brighton: 'She had never heard of Snowshill, but described it as if she were there: an upper room – 'tis late at night, in it a girl in a green dress of the 17th century, much agitated, paces up and down. She does not live there, and will not stay the night.' It was only some years later that Wade saw papers describing the Star Chamber case relating to the secret marriage of Ann Parsons.

Music Room
Seraphim

First Floor

Music Room

The musical instruments of the 18th and 19th century provide some fine examples of English craftsmanship. The inscription over the door means: 'Man is carried to heaven on the wings of music'. Ironically the angel hanging from the ceiling has no wings.

Left A selection of stringed instruments including guitar, harp-lute and double bass

The instruments are displayed in groups around the room, more or less in the order that would be found in a small orchestra. Thus on the left are the strings, in the centre the woodwind and brass, and on the right percussion. The keyed English guitar on the wall next to the door is thought to have belonged to Lady Hamilton, companion of Lord Nelson, alongside other plucked-string instruments. On the Turkoman rug are further stringed instruments, these ones played using a bow.

The woodwind section of the orchestra is well represented by the oboes and clarinets on the shelf, and the flutes on the wall are made from wood or ivory. Beside them hang two curious German flutes shaped like walking sticks. The three serpents, despite being made of wood and having finger holes rather than keys, are in fact classed as brass instruments.

In the corner, the percussion section is represented by several military drums and, above them, the smallest instrument in the room, a 19th-century triangle that was used by the Snowshill morris men. The brass instruments continue on the far side of the room with various horns, an English three-valve euphonium and a slide trumpet.

Seraphim

The collection in Seraphim is assembled from many distant lands, particularly Bali and Java. Many items here are unusual in that Charles Wade bought them on one of his rare trips overseas.

Wade remembered 'far-eastern markets, aglow with colour and tropical sun, strange sights and strange tongues', which may be where he purchased the three Balinese masks hanging on the wall, representing the evil demon queen Rangda of Balinese mythology. These masks would have been used in dances symbolizing battles in the perpetual struggle between good and evil.

Militaria

The six Indo-Persian shields are made from painted leather or steel and inlaid with gold. Accompanying them are six Indo-Persian helmets, mainly dating from the late 18th or early 19th century. Originally these had peacock feathers but these were removed as it was considered unlucky to have such feathers in the house. Other items include *kukri*, the knives traditionally carried by Ghurkha troops, and a two-edged double-curved sword from Ethiopia, which could be used to reach behind an opponent's shield.

Furniture

Tucked into the corner of the room, the Dutch box-bed dates from about 1680. On occasions, this was used by Wade's friends staying overnight at the manor. At its foot is a 17th-century Spanish *vargueno*, another example of Wade's fascination with cabinets of drawers for holding precious objects. On the left of the door, the two bow-fronted lacquered cupboards are English-made imitations of Chinese cabinets.

Left Indonesian theatre mask

Below Seraphim

Salamander and Dragon Nadir

Ground Floor

Salamander and Dragon

The gallery is named after the salamander of folklore that was thought to be able to live in fire. Through the railings can be seen Dragon, its own fiery association coming from the great fireplace.

Charles Wade often used these rooms for entertaining guests, using his collection of armour and weapons as theatrical props. Sections of the railings in Salamander open onto Dragon, where his audience would be seated. He frequently kept a fire in Dragon, creating a very smoky atmosphere, heightening the dramatic effect. His guests would hear stories from Wade and his friend Albert Richardson, including tales of the ghosts in the house – the monk on the stairs was a particular favourite. Imagine the guests sitting on the settle, with only the light from the fire, they hear the clanking of chains ... after which they were expected to take their candles and go upstairs to bed.

Around the walls are coats of arms intended to represent all of the owners and occupiers of the manor, but there are arms of some who had no direct connection with the manor, such as the first and second husbands of Catherine Parr (who was given the manor by her third husband, Henry VIII).

Amateur dramatics
Salamander and Dragon provided the stage for many performances by Charles Wade and his friends. The performers would dress up in wigs and cloaks and create a theatrical atmosphere by use of candles and lanterns, with glimpses of them through the railings to raise the audience's expectations. From the elevated position of Salamander, Richardson would read a scene from a play, acting all of the parts himself, dressed in costumes from Wade's collection. His grandson remembered many of the sketches, especially 'A Night at an Inn', which vividly described the discomfort and grime of the 18th century, including the full range of sound effects – blasts from the coaching horns, shouts from the ostlers and the barking of dogs. These performances often culminated in a sword fight, using real weapons from Wade's collection.

Right A touch of the dramatic in Salamander

Nadir

Originally this space held coal for the fire in Dragon. When he restored the house, Wade installed the barrel-vaulted ceiling as well as the inscription around the walls.

Around the cornice the inscription reads: 'A wise man is like a dial that being set right with the sun keepeth his true course in his compass. He measureth time and tempereth nature. He employeth reason and commandeth sense and envieth none.' Wade made each of the letters, which were cast in lead using wooden patterns.

Home security
The figure of a woman with a sword and a dog may look like a firescreen but is, in fact, a companion board, used to give the impression that someone was in the house.

Return through Dragon to reach the Lobby.

Lobby

Here is the original main door to the manor. The inscription over the cupboard to its left means 'I neither keep a dormouse as a servant nor a horseleech as a guest.'

Arresting items
Perhaps there was some security reason for keeping a collection of truncheons beside the door, but it seems unlikely in a sleepy Cotswold village. In the centre of these truncheons is a Bow Street Runner's tipstaff, the top of which unscrews to hold a warrant. Over the door are the bells from a wagon team which have been fashioned into a doorbell by Wade.

Now leave the house and cross the courtyard to the Priest's House.

Left **The crest of Imperial Russia**

Above **Room view of Dragon**

Priest's House

In recognition of the days when the manor belonged to Winchcombe Abbey, Charles Wade named this cottage after a priest's lodgings. At one time it had been used as a bake-house and a brew-house, later becoming farm buildings before Wade converted it to serve as his living quarters.

Wade would keep a fire in the kitchen throughout the year. Here he would sit in his favourite chair, the hall porter's chair on the left that would have offered protection against the draughts, perhaps to read his choice of authors, such as Jeffrey Farnol, or listen to the radio. He only accepted the presence of that modern device after the outbreak of the Second World War so he could hear the evening news but, as there was no mains electricity in the property, the batteries had to be recharged at the local garage.

The fire is supplied with air by a novel but practical arrangement of Wade's own devising – a pair of blacksmith's bellows in the adjoining workshop. These are operated by the cord which can be seen hanging above the other chair. The workshop, where Wade repaired and restored many of the items he acquired, can be glimpsed through the doorway to the right.

Cooking was generally not allowed at the manor, as it would have needed modern utensils. Mrs Hands (who lived in the cottages close by) prepared breakfast in the workshop. At other times, Wade made his own using a small spirit lamp to boil water for coffee or to cook some eggs which would be eaten with large slabs of bread. What he really enjoyed was guava jam or honey, which he ate by the spoonful.

Above Tools in Charles Wade's workshop in the Priest's House

Left The living room in the Priest's House

Above right Carved and painted wooden cat in the living room – the whiskers were replaced annually

Far right Charles Wade's bedroom

Furniture

Upstairs, the bedroom contains a Tudor box-bed but, in summertime, Wade preferred to sleep in a bedroom in the garden called 'The Jolly Roger'. Mrs Wade had her own bedroom in the rear of this building; the door can be seen at the end on the right but the room itself is not open to visitors. Amy Wade, Charles' mother, tried living at Snowshill in the later part of her life but rejected it as 'too medieval', preferring instead to stay with Commander Fred Hart in Chipping Campden.

Conveniences

The bathroom is opposite the bedroom and would have been reached by crossing an open passage – the current roof was installed during the renovation of Snowshill. Water was supplied to the bathroom by a hydraulic ram from the stream in the valley, heated by a boiler in the workshop. The 'thunderbox' toilet was the only such facility in the manor, so visitors would have to queue in the open to use it, even in the rain. This laid them open to harassment by the two peacocks that lived here.

After leaving the house, turn right to explore the garden.

Housekeeping

Meals were haphazard affairs. Charles Wade kept irregular hours, sometimes working for two days at a stretch, taking meals as he worked. Anthony Thomas remembered that 'Wade was the tidiest of men. Immediately on completing the smallest job … everything (was) made clean and tidy.' The house itself might be filled with smoke from the fire in Dragon but the metallic objects were kept burnished and sparkling clean. Edwin Lutyens noted that 'the large amount of brass work and other metals are as bright as the sun'.

'Outdoor Rooms'

'A garden is an extension of the house, a series of outdoor rooms.' This precisely describes the garden designed and constructed at Snowshill Manor. The basis for the design is a scheme developed by M. H. Baillie Scott, an architect Charles Wade knew from his Hampstead days.

Pictured Snowshill garden is arranged as a series of outdoor rooms

Wade had been developing his ideas for gardens long before he came to Snowshill. When he first saw the house it stood 'in the midst of a wilderness of chaos'. Yet it presented 'a happy chance to create a garden of interest'. So he planned the garden as a series of outdoor rooms or, as he called them, courts.

The house stands at the top of a steep slope falling to the west, so the first thing was to provide a secure base, 'to lose the feeling it gave of being about to slide into the depths of the valley'. This was achieved by terracing and a series of retaining walls.

The land had been neglected, nettles covered the whole area from the house right down to the kitchen garden, which itself was covered in debris. The only wall still standing was the one on the south side of the Orchard. The lower part of the garden was a swamp due to the springs emerging from the hillside.

The court on the south side of the house had first to be levelled and then connected with the long terrace at the lower level by new steps. The inner courtyard (between the manor and the Priest's House) was cleared and levelled, and new walls and paving installed. The garden itself was laid out on the slope to the west of the house. Baillie Scott's design used terracing to establish levels, each of which was then divided into rooms with their own features, making use of existing farm buildings to add structure to the plan.

Left Wade's notebook showing his plan for the garden

Mackay Hugh Baillie Scott (1865–1945)
A fellow architect, M. H. Baillie Scott developed the concept of the integrated interior of a building, designing the furniture for most of his buildings, considering the client's use of their own furniture 'incongruous if the rooms themselves are architecturally beautiful'. His integrated approach extended to exteriors, considering 'for many architects, a well-designed garden was almost as important as a well-designed house. We can hardly do better than to try and reproduce some of the beauties of the old English gardens, with their terraces and courts and dusky yew hedges which makes such a splendid background to the bright colours of flowers.'

Arts and Crafts influences

With so much work to be done to the garden, Charles Wade could give full rein to his ideas. In keeping with the Arts and Crafts Movement, he made use of local materials, local craftsmen and traditional methods, complemented by key features he commissioned for the garden.

The purpose of a garden, as he saw it, was to provide an appropriate setting for thinking and resting, for enjoying the songs of the birds and to provide food for the insects – 'a place for pretty thoughts and soft musings'.

Below Well Court under construction

Light and shade

Wade had clear ideas about the designs of the outdoor rooms. There would be variety and balance, formal and informal – 'sunny ones contrasting with shady ones and different courts for varying moods'. The plan of the garden, especially the hard surfaces, was much more important than the flowers: 'Walls, steps and alleyways give a permanent setting, so that it is pleasant and orderly in both summer and winter.' At the same time, 'mystery is most valuable in design' so Wade's garden would not show everything at once. Rather than having a succession of flowerbeds, he preferred to achieve 'broad effects of light and shade' whilst using unbroken stretches of grass. Vistas, whilst important, must be completed with definite, terminal features.

'Here be delights that will fetch the day about from sun to sun.'

Days Far Away. Memories of Charles Paget Wade (1883–1956)

Use of colour

As to the use of furniture, Wade detested deck chairs but thought that 'well-designed garden seats can be a useful addition to a garden if carefully placed'. Artificial colour must only be used with care: 'Never paint a "nature" green – turquoise is the most satisfactory colour, a foil to the grass and foliage.' In fact his own creation, Wade blue, is subtly different from turquoise. The final touch would be inscriptions 'in good lettering', which would add interest to the garden. Many such inscriptions can be seen around the garden.

Even though he believed he could make 'a delightful garden … in which flowers play a very small part', Wade was not averse to using flowers, providing their colours were suited to the grey colour of the weathered Cotswold stone. Thus he selected delphiniums, lupins, larkspur and lavender to provide blues, mauves and purples, with salmon and cream tones as secondary colours but only sparing use of bright yellows and reds.

The garden today

Starting out from the corner of the Priest's House, there is a statue of St George and the Dragon, commissioned by Charles Wade from a Tyrolean craftsman, A. Dapre. It is a copy in teak of a statue in the Victoria and Albert Museum, faithful in every detail except its size – the original is only 0.56 metres high.

Armillary Court

From here there is a choice of routes. The main path leads down the steps, through the avenue of yew trees to the Armillary Court, named after the armillary sphere which is on top of a stone pillar at its centre (other armillary spheres may be seen in Admiral). This pillar was made from a gate-post found in the farmyard. On the right, the bronze mask in the terrace wall forms a water spout. This was made for Wade by Eileen Heenan Cosomati, R.A., copied from one in the V&A; it is fed by a spring from the cellar beneath Admiral. Further round this court you will find the pond and Wolf's Cove, the model village which Wade set out here each summer. For many years, the model buildings were brought out and put into place each spring, and then put back under cover in the autumn.

Left Teak statue of St George and the Dragon

Right Looking through a stone archway into the Armillary Court

The Jolly Roger

To the left of the Wolf's Cove pond is a little room that Wade called 'The Jolly Roger', constructed from the roof space of the Sancta Maria Byre. In summer Wade used this cabin as a bedroom and would plunge into the pool every morning for a bracing wash.

Well Court

Returning to the main path from the manor, follow the steps down to the next court which has, at its centre, a Venetian stone well-head, giving it the name of Well Court. On the left, the 24-hour garden clock features astrological devices and inscriptions from the teachings of St Bernard of Clairvaux. This clock is called the Nychthemeron, Greek for 'night and day'. All of the metalwork for this was made by George Hart, a silversmith in Chipping Campden.

Right above The Jolly Roger in the roof space above the Sancta Maria Byre

Right The Nychthemeron

By the byre

At the far end of Well Court, an old cow-byre houses some of the items from Charles Wade's collection that were too large to fit in the house. A shrine to the Virgin Mary is mounted in the gable, from which the byre takes its name – Sancta Maria. This statue was carved in teak by A. Dapre, the same craftsman who made the statue of St George.

Inside Sancta Maria, two hand-operated Merryweather fire pumps show what would have been involved in fighting a parish fire in the middle of the 19th century. They still have some of the leather hoses and hooks that would have been used to tackle blazes. On the other side of the byre is a Flemish chariot. The large press was once used for making the local cheese, Double Gloucester. Looking up you can see a window into Jolly Roger. Behind this byre, the Elder Court is lined with Elder trees.

Right View of the Long Border leading down to the Dovecote

The Dovecote

Further round Well Court, you will find another byre and, beyond that, the Dovecote, the one that can be seen from the Grey Room in the manor. In the Dovecote are nesting boxes for 380 birds; it is still home to a flock of white doves. The stone tablet on the wall is inscribed with a poem by Henry Van Dyke: 'Hours fly, flowers die, new days, new ways, pass by, love stays.' The byre also holds some of the models that were made for Wolf's Cove, together with photographs of the village in its heyday in Wade's time.

The Kitchen Garden

Beside the Dovecote a path leads down to the Kitchen Garden, passing between a pair of stone piers to a gate which replaced the old farm wall. The piers are topped with stone balls cut by a local stonemason. Over the gate the inscription reads: 'A garden sweet enclosed with walles strong,/The Arbours and Ayles so pleasant and so dulce.'

Stonework

Returning to Well Court, the line of steps can be seen stretching straight up to the manor house. Wade tried to cut the names of the Thirteen Virtues in the risers of these steps but found the stone was unsuitable after his first few attempts, which can still just be seen. An alternative route back to the house is up the steps beside the Nychthemeron. On the upper level, Wade cut a map of his horoscope.

Below A detail of the model village Wolf's Cove

The world of Wolf's Cove

Whilst living in Hampstead, Charles Wade built one of the first model villages designed for use outdoors, based on a Cotswold village, which he called 'Fladbury'. Later, when laying out the gardens at Snowshill, he incorporated the village but changed its name to 'Wolf's Cove' and added a port. The name was taken from a hulk he had seen and sketched in Ipswich harbour. In *English Journey* (1934) J. B. Priestley recorded his pleasure at seeing the village: 'The miniature seaport … has a proper harbour in one of the ponds of the garden. It has its quay, its fleet of ships, its lighthouse, its railway system with station, sidings and all, its inn, main street and side streets, thatched cottages and actual living woods.' John Betjeman endowed the village with real characters to such good effect that his article about it in *The Architectural Review* (1931) persuaded at least one reader that the village really did exist!

Finishing the effect

Simple cottage garden plants dominate the borders, as they have always done, with variable but ordered planting. The colours tend to be soft ones, as Charles Wade preferred, with the odd splash of colour – 'larkspurs lifting turquoise spires, bluer than the sorcerer's fires'.

Just as Wade had very clearly defined ideas on presentation, the garden team today strive to keep as faithfully as possible to his scheme. They are assisted in this endeavour by the volumes of notes Wade left behind. The garden covers an area of about 0.8 hectares (2 acres) and much is as Wade conceived and later bequeathed to the Trust. Some of the box and grapevines in the garden are from the original planting, as are the yews in Armillary Court.

Although Wade may have been more interested in garden design than in horticulture – 'the plan of the garden is much more important than the flowers in it' – there is much for the plantsman to enjoy.

Right One of Wade's favourite views was looking up the steps from the Dovecote towards the house

Flowering plants

Wade did not care much for the formal Rose Garden calling it 'a snare and delusion; it sounds much more attractive than it looks'. Rather he preferred that roses were kept out of sight for use just as cut flowers. The one exception was climbing roses, but this was as much for the deep shade created by their overhang as for their flowers.

Fruit and vegetables

Today the Kitchen Garden provides a regular supply of tasty salads, fruits and vegetables for the restaurant. The Orchard features a range of traditional varieties of fruit, having been replanted in the early 1990s with local varieties of apples from Gloucestershire, Worcestershire and Herefordshire. Below the greenhouse, pear trees and damson trees flourish beside the Nut Walk.

Favourite views

Wade had a number of favourite views in his garden, four in particular.

One is down the grass terrace from the Long Border to the yew hedge at the end. Another is from the Dovecote, looking up the flight of steps to the house, with the chimney towering against the sky.

To share in another view favoured by Wade, stand by the lily pool in Well Court with the reflection of the turquoise-blue shrine, and look through the gates of Sancta Maria Byre to the Elder Court. Wade described the Elder Court as 'a cool and fragrant shade, an enticing tangle of stems of aged elders, the deep shades dappled with vivid green lights.'

And finally, the approach to the house from the secondhand bookshop provides the contrast of the shady courtyard with the open and sunny courtyard beyond.

Above left
The orchard

Above right The second-hand bookshop

Below The garden inscription by Wade

Continuity of care

As with many other aspects of his life, Charles Wade's attitude towards the management of the garden was strongly influenced by his memories of growing up in Suffolk.

The gardener in his father's house had been so passionate about his work that it bordered on the obsessive. As Wade recalled, 'It became his garden in which we were allowed to walk…. If asked to move a plant, we were always told it was the wrong time of the year, or the plant was too old or too young.'

So, when he established the garden at Snowshill, Wade determined that the garden would be his rather than his gardener's. He found that one of the local labourers involved in restoring the house knew nothing about gardening (except for cabbages and cauliflowers). This man seemed ideally qualified for the position of gardener. Wade also liked his name (Hodge) and his hat, which was a cloth hat 'like a keeper's'. As a result, Wade hired Hodge who remained the gardener at Snowshill for 37 years. Hodge was willing to move plants 'in spite of the time of the year, in spite of their age' and, incredibly, they flourished. But for all his years of good service, Hodge was fired when he answered back to an order given to him by Wade's wife Mary.

Notwithstanding Hodge's dismissal, gardening at Snowshill had a family tradition. Victor Hands took over from Hodge, but when he retired at the age of 73, the job passed to Hodge's son Bob, who worked at Snowshill for 15 years. In a book of reminiscences, *Cotswold Born 'n' Bred: My life at Snowshill*, Bob Hodge wrote that, between him and his father, they planted practically all the trees and shrubs growing in the garden today.

Following tradition

Since Bob Hodge's retirement in 1979, there have been only five other gardeners-in-charge at Snowshill, all of whom endeavoured to follow Wade's philosophy. One tradition is the lack of any plant labelling.

Natural principles

As far as pests are concerned, few aphids like the exposure or the altitude of the Snowshill site, so these are not as much of a problem as might be the case lower down the hill. Fungal disease is addressed, as far as possible, by prompt removal and destruction of infected material. The cottage garden plants that dominate the borders are generally free of major problems.

The landscaping needs less attention than the plants. One change that has been made is to replace the soft Cotswold stone, used for paving, with a more durable stone.

Opposite Bob Hodge followed in his father's footsteps

Below The vegetable garden with newly installed raised beds

Craftsmanship

Some ever would be where they're not,
Would ever have that they've not got.
True Happiness – contented mind
Sufficient near at hand will find.
Absorbing interests lie all round,
Will by observant mind be found.
Create something however small,
There lies the truest joy of all,
When brain and hand together strive,
Real happiness becomes alive.
In the pursuit the pleasure lies,
The how and wherefore to devise.
Though vision dreamed will far excel
The work achieved, yet it is well,
To have attempted is not in vain.
Failure urges one on again.
Great craftsman, asked once to decide
Which was his greatest work, replied
Simply with these two words "My next".
For "ever better" was his text.

Charles Paget Wade (1883–1956)

Right A fine finish on the
finger plate of the door of
the Grey Room